KT-524-021

Caribbean Islands

Alice Harman

Explore the world with **Popcorn** - your complete first non-fiction library.

Look out for more titles in the Popcorn range. All books have the same format of simple text and striking images. Text is carefully matched to the pictures to help readers to identify and understand key vocabulary.
www.waylandbooks.co.uk/popcorn

Published in paperback in 2013 by Wayland
Copyright © Wayland 2013

Wayland
Hachette Children's Books
338 Euston Road
London NW1 3BH

Wayland Australia
Level 17/207 Kent Street
Sydney NSW 2000

Produced for Wayland by
White-Thomson Publishing Ltd
www.wtpub.co.uk
+44 (0)843 208 7460

Editor: Alice Harman
Designer: Clare Nicholas
Picture researcher: Alice Harman
Series consultant: Kate Ruttle
Design concept: Paul Cherrill

British Library Cataloging in Publication Data
Harman, Alice, 1987-
   Caribbean Islands. -- (Countries)(Popcorn)
   1. West Indies--Juvenile literature.
   I. Title II. Series
   917.2'9-dc23

ISBN: 978 0 7502 7944 4

Wayland is a division of Hachette Children's Books,
an Hachette UK company.
www.hachette.co.uk

Printed and bound in China

Picture/Illustration Credits: Peter Bull: 23; Stefan Chabluk: 4; Corbis: Kevin Fletcher 12, Peter Adams 13, Blaine Harrington 21; Dreamstime: Desertdiver imprint and 7, Cphoto title page and 8, Gartharchibald 17(tl); Getty: AFP 9; Jenny Matthews: 18; Photoshot: Steve Vidler cover; www.plazalasamericas.net: 15; Shutterstock: RoxyFer 5, Lucia Pitter 6, Eugene Moerman 10, rj lerich 16 and 17(tr), Vladimir Melnik 16(t), Lisa F. Young 17(br), MAT 19, Salim October 20; Travel Library: James Davies 14; WTPix: 11.

Every effort has been made to clear copyright. Should there be any inadvertent omission, please apply to the publisher for rectification.

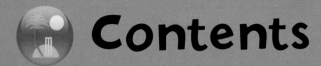 Contents

Where are the
    Caribbean Islands?   4

Land and sea   6

The weather   8

Town and country   10

Homes   12

Shopping   14

Food   16

Sport   18

Holidays and festivals   20

Flags   22

Make a coral reef   23

Glossary   24

Index   24

Where are the Caribbean Islands?

Here is a map of the Caribbean.

There are 28 island countries

in the Caribbean.

UNITED
STATES
OF
AMERICA

Atlantic

Ocean

THE
BAHAMAS

Nassau

TURKS &
CAICOS
ISLANDS

VIRGIN
ISLANDS

BARBUDA

San
Juan

ANTIGUA

Havana

CUBA

DOMINICAN
REPUBLIC

PUERTO
RICO

ST. KITTS
& NEVIS

MONTSERRAT

HAITI

GUADELOUPE

DOMINICA

CAYMAN
ISLANDS

Port-au-Prince

San
Domingo

MARTINIQUE

ST. LUCIA

Kingston

ST. VINCENT

BARBADOS

JAMAICA

GRENADA

TOBAGO

TRINIDAD

Caribbean

NETHERLANDS
ANTILLES

HONDURAS

ARUBA

Sea

NICARAGUA

VENEZUELA

COSTA
RICA

COLOMBIA

PANAMA

BRAZIL

NORTH
AMERICA

EUROPE

AFRICA

SOUTH
AMERICA

Cuba is the largest island in the Caribbean, and has the biggest population. Its capital is Havana. People in Cuba speak Spanish.

Havana is famous for its old cars and buildings.

Land and sea

Caribbean islands often have mountains or volcanoes. The mountainsides and lower slopes are covered with thick forest.

The two Piton mountains in St Lucia were formed by ancient volcanoes.

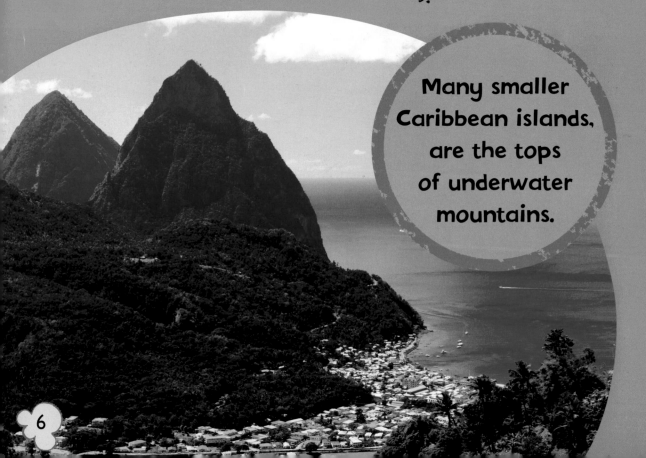

Many smaller Caribbean islands, are the tops of underwater mountains.

The Caribbean Sea is one of
the largest seas in the world.
There are many underwater coral
reefs around the Caribbean islands.

More than 75 different corals and
700 kinds of fish live in Caribbean reefs.

The weather

The dry season lasts from December to May. It is not so rainy at this time of year. Many tourists visit the Caribbean in this season.

Coconut palm trees grow along this sandy beach in Martinique.

The rainy season is from June to November. There are sometimes tropical storms and hurricanes.

Rain is often heavier in the mountains than by the coast.

There are normally eight hurricanes in the **Caribbean** every year.

Town and country

On some Caribbean islands, such as Puerto Rico and the Cayman Islands, almost all the people live in towns or cities.

San Juan is the capital of Puerto Rico. It is famous for its colourful buildings.

On islands such as Saint Lucia and Grenada, most people live in the countryside. Houses often have big gardens for growing food and keeping animals.

This Saint Lucian man is growing a leafy vegetable called elephant's ear.

Homes

Cities on Caribbean islands often have new and expensive flats in the centre. Cheaper houses are normally further out, around the edge of the city.

This family home looks over Santiago de Cuba, the second largest city in Cuba.

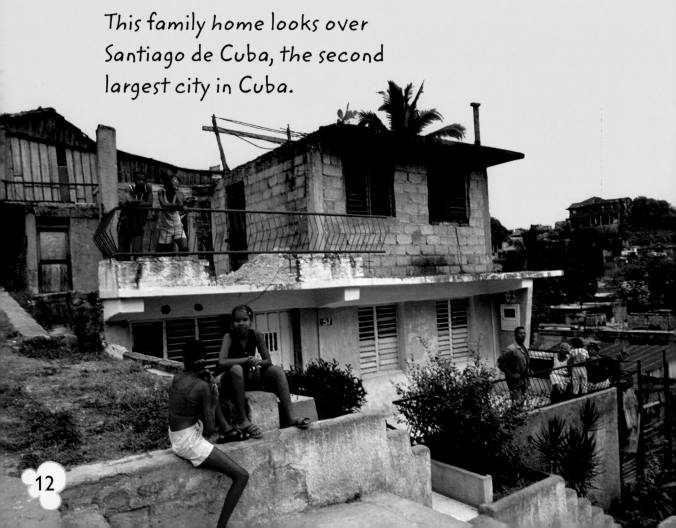

In Barbados, wooden houses built on stone blocks are called chattel houses. They can be moved to different places because they are not built into the ground.

Chattel houses are often painted in pale colours to help keep them cool.

The oldest chattel houses were built more than 200 years ago.

Shopping

Many Caribbean people shop for fresh fruit, vegetables, nuts and spices at outdoor markets.

People at this market in St. George's, Grenada, use umbrellas to shelter from the hot sun.

Most big cities on Caribbean islands have
at least one indoor shopping centre.
There are sometimes restaurants
and a cinema in these centres.

Plaza Las Américas in San Juan, Puerto Rico,
is the largest shopping centre in the Caribbean.

Food

Fruits such as guavas and mangoes grow throughout the year. The Caribbean Sea is full of fish that are delicious to eat. They can be grilled or baked.

red snapper

This fisherman is about to go fishing out at sea.

Different Caribbean islands have their own traditional dishes. Some foods, like these below, are popular on many of the islands.

Guava cheese is a sweet made with guava, sugar and cinnamon.

Jonnycake is a kind of fried flat bread that is enjoyed as a snack.

All over the Caribbean, this everyday meal of grilled meat, rice and beans and fried plantain is eaten.

 # Sport

Football is one of the most popular sports in the Caribbean. Teams from Caribbean islands play in the Caribbean Cup.

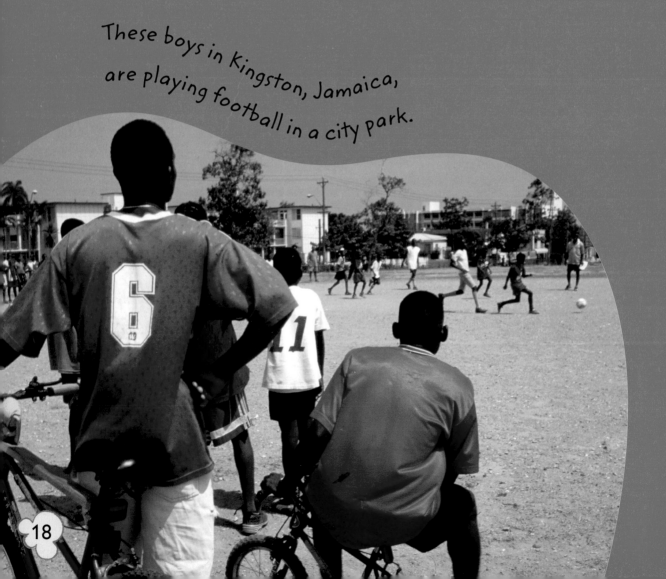

These boys in Kingston, Jamaica, are playing football in a city park.

Cricket is also very popular on Caribbean islands. The world-famous West Indies team has players from all over the Caribbean.

The West Indies cricket team has won the Cricket World Cup twice.

The West Indies is another name for the Caribbean.

Holidays and festivals

Emancipation Day celebrates the end of slavery, and the freedom of the Caribbean people. It is celebrated on 1 August, or the first Monday in August, each year.

On Emancipation Day, people in Trinidad and Tobago dress up to celebrate their culture and remember their history.

Many Caribbean islands celebrate Carnival on one day in February each year. There are parades in the street with music and colourful costumes.

It can take months to make costumes for Carnival, and there are prizes for the best design.

Flags

Each country in the Caribbean has its own flag. These flags are often brightly coloured. Try painting the flags below and make a colourful display.

Aruba

Dominica

Cuba

Barbados

Antigua & Barbuda

Jamaica

Make a coral reef

You will need:
- scissors · glue · 2 paper plates
- blue coloured paper
- white paper · crayons
- sticky tape

There are lots of coral reefs in the seas around the Caribbean. They are full of brightly coloured plants and fish.

1. Turn one paper plate upside down and draw a circle around the bottom of the plate. Cut along the circle you drew (ask an adult to start off cutting).

2. Put the cut-out circle on the blue paper and draw around it. Cut out the circle of blue paper and stick it to the inside of the other plate.

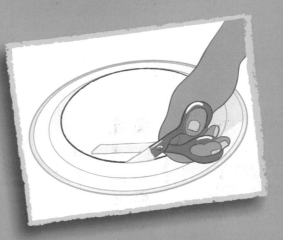

3. Draw and colour in some different sea creatures. Cut these out and stick them onto the blue paper background.

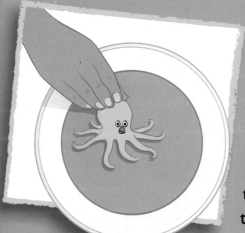

4. Use small pieces of sticky tape to stick the inside edges of the two plates together. Look through the hole and see your own coral reef!

23

Glossary

capital the city where the government of the country meets

charcoal a material made from wood and used for cooking

coral a hard substance made of the skeletons of tiny sea creatures

coral reef an underwater shelf made of corals

hurricane a storm with a very strong wind

parade when people walk together in the streets to celebrate something

plantain a vegetable that grows in the Caribbean and looks like a big, green banana

slavery when people are forced to work for no money and are not allowed to leave

traditional a belief, art or way of doing something that has been a part of a culture or society for a long time

volcano a mountain with an opening at the top where hot liquid rock from underground can flow out

Index

Barbados 13
beaches 8

Carnival 21
Cayman Islands 10
chattel houses 13
coasts 9
coral reefs 7
cricket 19

festivals 20-21
fishing 16

food 11, 14, 16-17
football 18

Grenada 11, 14

houses and homes 12-13
hurricanes 9

Martinique 8
mountains 6, 9

Puerto Rico 10, 15

Saint Lucia 6, 11
shopping 14-15
sport 18-19

Trinidad and Tobago 20
tourists 8
towns and cities 10, 12

volcanoes 6

weather 8-9